500 Science Fiction

and

Fantasy Writing Prompts

BY: JULIE WENZEL

500 Science Fiction and Fantasy Writing Prompts

Copyright © 2016 by Julie Wenzel

ISBN-13: 978-1537093345

ISBN-10: 1537093347

To contact the author visit:

www.jmwenzel.com

Author: Julie Wenzel
Cover Art by: Julie Wenzel

TABLE OF CONTENTS

JULIE WENZEL

FOREWORD

Inspiration can hit us at any time of the day without warning. Dreams, quotes, sounds, and life events are all ways inspiration can creep into our lives. That sudden jolt of adrenaline from an idea is an amazing feeling.

But what happens when ideas run dry?

I can relate to the dreaded writer's block. If you allow yourself to succumb to it for too long you could even end up giving up writing completely. To avoid long-term writer's block, it is important to just write *anything*. What you write doesn't always have to contribute to any long-term project. What matters most is that you keep exercising your writing skills.

Any amount of writing is a positive thing, no matter the word count.

Prompts are a healthy way to keep your writing sharp. I hope these story starters can help you generate some elaborate ideas.

Don't ever let yourself surrender to writer's block.

Weeks will turn into months. Months will turn into years.

Write every single day if possible. If there's ever a time you are out of ideas for a story, refer to this book. All prompts are free for you to use for your next project, no matter the size. No attribution is required.

Have fun!

HOW TO USE THIS BOOK

You may use this book in any way that fits your writing needs. You can use these ideas for a novel, script, painting, or anything you make for personal or commercial use. You cannot use these writing prompts in a stand-alone manner such as using these exact prompts in a prompt book of your own.

No attribution is required if any of these prompts inspire you to write a large piece of commercial work. Of course, I'd love to hear from you if this book really inspired you somehow.

Whatever you decide to take away from this book is up to you. My ultimate goal here is to inspire you.

This book contains several different style prompts.

- Short one sentence prompts.

- Prompts with a question or two at the end.

- Long prompts similar to an excerpt from a book.

- Prompts that read like a book blurb.

I did this purposely because everyone gets inspired in different ways.

Some of the prompts you can expect to see in this book:

- Medieval Times

- Artificial Intelligence

- Mermaids

- Ancient Artifacts

- Dragons

- Aliens

- Government Conspiracies

- Space Travel

- Wormholes

Some prompts may be a little more humorous and childlike while others are on the serious side. Science fiction and fantasy prompts are mixed together in this book. I find that there can be overlap between the two genres if a writer so desires.

Even though this is a science fiction and fantasy prompt book, don't hesitate to twist what you write into another genre such as paranormal, horror, mystery thriller, or romance.

This book is about *you* and staying inspired.

Because this book contains 500 prompts, there is enough content for you to write one prompt a day for over a year.

A few ways to use this book:

- Think of a random number or roll some dice. Find that number in the book and write about it.

- Have someone else choose a number for you.

- Use these as a daily classroom exercise for your students.

- Make a game or a contest with these prompts. Choose a prompt for a group of writers to use as a starting point. Vote on the best story and award prizes.

- Start from 1 and work all the way to 500, forcing yourself to write each and every prompt.

- Write short flash fiction inspired by the prompt.

- Write a whole page or chapter.

- Write an entire novel with the prompts for fun or to sell.

- Combine several prompts into a single epic novel.

Artists can use these prompts to inspire their artwork.

Video game developers can use this book to incorporate ideas into their game such as magic systems, worlds, characters, or full plots.

There are no rules to this book.

Use this book to exercise your writing, come up with new ideas, or enhance your already existing stories.

SECTION 1: PROMPTS 1 - 49

1. Write about a bounty hunter that doesn't hunt humans, as there are very few left. Instead, he is paid to kill off the strongest and most intelligent robots that roam the planet.

2. Magic is finally proven to be real. However, it is also found to be useless. Describe what kind of magic is discovered and how it is used.

3. Write about a medieval knight that is sent forward in time to help save a post-apocalyptic society.

4. Describe a brand-new sport that can only be played at zero gravity. What are the rules?

5. In a last-ditch effort to become famous, an aspiring actress decides to transform into a cat. She hopes to build a following similar to all the famous online cats. Write about her new career.

6. Eight astronauts have their personalities programmed into cyborgs that will be sent off into space to look for habitable land. After one hundred years of searching the stars, the cyborgs have

found another place for humans to live. When they return, all of the original astronauts are dead, but the grandchildren still live. The cyborgs sit down with the families and tell stories of their adventures. Tell the stories of the cyborgs that have taken on the personalities of the eight astronauts.

7. There have been many paranormal activity phone applications created, but this is the first one that has a proven 100% success rate. What happens when everyone decides to download the application and try it out for themselves?

8. Write a story about an epic battle between two kingdoms in the point of view of a warhorse.

9. As a way to increase their chances of victory against a dark lord, high wizards attempt to give every human some form of magical ability. However, this backfires on everyone. What happens?

10. You have spent the last two years covering up the fact that you transferred yourself into a high school of wizards, alchemists, and dragon tamers. You are now required to bring your parents to the next conference or be forced to go back to public schools. As a star student, you know it is time to come out and tell the truth to your parents. What is your next course of action?

11. You are a detective about to crack a case. One day, you discover that you have been cloned. What's worse, is your clone is trying to undo all the progress you have made with the case.

12. The men lined up in a processional march, one by one towards the cathedral. What was inside the cathedral that brought so many?

13. When the king died, the rain finally stopped and the clouds parted. How was his life connected to the weather?

14. The witch of the white ocean has been perched on top of an iceberg for fifty years. Ships always avoid nearing the iceberg to steer clear of her powers. You are a passenger on a ship that has suddenly changed direction. You are heading straight for her.

15. You discover the cat lady in your neighborhood to be the one who is trolling the internet about government conspiracies. One day, you decide to confront her. But just as you are about to knock on her front door, your cell phone rings in your pocket. The caller? Somehow the name, "The Cat Lady" is already programmed into your phone.

16. The faster her heart beats, the more her skin glows. What is causing this phenomenon?

17. She took it upon herself to foster two newborn dragons and nurse them back to health. Never did she worry about what kind of beasts they could become when they were full grown. Her immediate worry was the journey she had ahead of her. In order for the newborns to survive, she would have to go on an expedition in search for a rare food only mentioned in ancient books.

18. A war is initiated between mermaids and humans. To protect the shoreline, mermaids hire an army of elemental sorcerers that can manipulate the sand. Why are the two sides at war?

19. Write about a cute creature that arrives on the planet Earth to protect a young girl from danger.

20. Homeless people are given the human equivalent of a turtle shell to live in. Describe the advantages or repercussions of this new lifestyle for the homeless.

21. Tell a story about three kingdoms that are said to have been swallowed up by a colossal serpent. No outsider has ever been able to enter the serpent alive. How do these three kingdoms continue to function in the belly of the beast?

22. The knight descends from the mountain with only his horse and a bag of wheat. Due to starvation of the land, the bag of wheat is worth more than a full set of armor and a new weapon. How will he protect the frail bag of wheat from the elements, thieves, and beasts as he makes his way to the next village to sell it?

23. Write about a pilgrimage of a mage that must tame a beast in order to be taught his final spell. What is the final spell? What kind of creature does he tame?

24. What would a reality TV show be like in the year 2070?

25. Write about a world where it is illegal to take your own photos. Any photo taken must be approved of first.

26. A lone farmer begins his harvest, pulling up his turnip plants. The last plant he uncovers is not a turnip, but a ticking mechanical egg. Numbers and lights flash all around its circular form. What happens next?

27. Statues that resemble the gods are built equal distance from each other on the sea shore. These statues have been enchanted by the most powerful wizards in history in order to keep tidal waves and weather at bay. One day all of the statues have mysteriously disappeared. Where did they go?

28. The arranged marriage was the event of the century. For the first time, magic and technology alliances would be made between a beloved king and a queen from the stars.

29. Biohazard waste spills throughout the flooded city. Anyone who walks through the flood waters suddenly is able to fly. It doesn't take long for the entire city to take flight. How does this change how the city is run?

30. You purchase a used self-driving car to save on cost. Frustrated at all the setup instructions, you punch the main console. Somehow you end up in a backend panel with options not found in the manual anywhere. Several modes are listed: *Self-destruct*, *Assassinate*, and *Find Person*. Do you call the manufacturer, the police, or investigate on your own why the buttons are programmed in there?

31. A patient during your last week before retirement enters your office complaining about an open wound that absorbs anything it touches. When he takes the bandage off his shoulder, a black void with tiny sparkles inside is revealed. He grabs your pen and sticks it in the hole where it instantly disappears. You decide to postpone your retirement in order to get to the bottom of this anomaly.

32. Write about a waitress that discovers her own superpowers after becoming irritated with rude customers.

33. Write a futuristic version of Cinderella. In this version, Cinderella's feet can reshape to any shoe size. Tell her story.

34. Astronauts discover artifacts on the moon that some believe are over 600 years old. How did they get there?

35. The room was filled with thousands of books, but all the pages were blank.

36. The mutant shark roamed the floors of the coral reef for years, waiting for the right time to make his ascend to the shores. Before he became a mutant, he never understood loneliness. Now, each day seemed lonelier than the last.

37. The only way for him to extract all the extra magic building inside of him was by jumping in a big pool of water. The consequences of too much magic in his system was not pretty.

38. I am heading to the bottom of a catacomb with my crew where a four-hundred-year-old witch is being held captive. I was chosen to learn everything she knows. From there, I must teach what I learn to a handful of people I trust. My biggest fear is that I'll end up just like her.

39. The old man only makes animal sounds, yet he is the wisest of them all.

40. Aliens enter Earth and seem to come in peace. Everything appears to be going smoothly until they decide to dominate the world and force everyone back into a time period they are completely obsessed with. What time period do the aliens force Earthlings to relive?

41. After the dust settles and the two kingdoms kill each other off, a young survivor crawls out of his hiding spot and finds a way to live. Years later, he appoints himself as king and seeks out other humans to live in the new world. But because he has been alone for so long, his social skills are lacking and many are turned off by his animal-like behavior. Write about this unusual king.

42. Underwater weddings with mermaids become the next huge fad in the industry. Write about a catastrophe that quickly brings this trend to an end.

43. We invited a non-human foreign exchange student from another galaxy over for the year. My 7-year-old is trying to explain to him what Halloween is all about and why people dress up. Now they are going over costume ideas together, and I am cracking up at all of the exchange student's ideas.

44. Before the homeless man took his last breath, he tells a passerby that he is God and the world is doomed. The next day proves his words to be true.

45. You purchase an old jukebox that is said to be broken at an antique store. After returning home and testing it out, you discover each button plays a song of magic only you can hear.

46. Magic is controlled by a sorceress' ability to connect with plant life. Roses control fire. Lilies control water. Trees control strength. Write about a sorceress that is determined to master it all.

47. A spaceship crash lands in the year 2065 in the suburbs of New York City. At first, the government, NASA, and other independent researchers close off the area for further investigation. After 50 years, they become bored of the ship and just sell it to the highest bidder. The ship is turned into an upscale restaurant. 15 years into the business, random lights and terminals turn on in the middle of a busy dinner service. The ship starts to ascend into the sky for the first time since it landed 65 years ago with customers inside.

48. A woman is found on the side of the road nearly dead. The paramedics arrive and load her up in the back of the ambulance. On their way to the hospital, the woman wakes up and transports everyone in the ambulance back to her world. Who is she? Where does she take them?

49. You discover you are able to read social media posts minutes before they are published. It has become a way for you to predict the future. An anonymous hacker soon discovers your ability and plans to stop you. Realizing all the people you could help save, an online battle between you and the hacker begins.

SECTION 2: PROMPTS 50 - 99

50. I refused to proceed until he could promise to take me back in time and fix what he had done.

51. Parents buy their son a robot that can tutor in any subject. The boy absorbs so much knowledge from the robot tutor that he learns how to reprogram him from the ground up. How does the boy change the robot?

52. You are given a magical book that grants any wish to come true, as long as it is written in the book. As a kind person, you want to grant people many wishes. You soon discover that having too many wishes granted at once causes more harm than good because many conflict with one another. How have these wishes influenced the world around you?

53. Write about a street urchin that teaches herself the art of magic in order to feed herself. Eventually, her abilities take her to something much more.

54. Write about a goddess that enjoys making practical jokes on humans on Earth.

55. Creatures from Greek mythology begin to appear out of nowhere in all of the largest tourist attractions around the world including the Statue of Liberty, the Louvre, and the Taj Mahal. Where did they come from?

56. A kindergarten student brings a strange interstellar object to show and tell. The government is called and the school is quarantined. Write about what was brought to school. How did the student get her hands on it?

57. Magic is regulated by the government. A neutralizer is emitted into the air and vents all across the world to keep magic at bay. To reverse the process legally, people must purchase a taxable drink that temporarily blocks the effects of the neutralizer. How is this drink distributed?

58. When the world was new, humans lived closely with their gods. Eventually, the gods wanted to move on from the humans and build a new world. Humans were given a choice: immediate use of magic or a progressive growth in knowledge so they could eventually follow the gods to their new planet. What do the humans choose?

59. Write about the Elemental Master of Earth. Though once said to be of peace and harmony, his mind increasingly turns evil. His progressive darkness can be compared to a form of dementia caused by age.

60. Every time the train made a stop at the next station there was only one person waiting, but they never got on. After a while, you realize it is the same person every time.

61. The king announces that his heir will not be any of his sons, but instead his loyal canine companion. Everyone laughs at first until the king dies and his wolf stands up on his two back legs and claims the throne.

62. I love my first apartment. It's not too far from a well-known commercial wormhole. There's no telling what'll come through it. My favorite pizza delivery place uses it to get to me. But one morning, something came through the hole that I wasn't happy about at all.

63. The president decides to risk his life and fight in a war no one believes in. When he arrives on the battlefield, he rides up on a dinosaur exclaiming, "Will you follow me now?"

64. A litter of puppies is destined to die without special help. Their only hope is the fire breathing dragon down the road.

65. Write about an old witch that has the power to control insects. By the time you hear the bees that circle her head, it is too late to save yourself.

66. As she blinks with such melancholy, I witness the eye of the beast behind her pupils.

67. The longer she stared out the window of the attic, the more the other world within the glass pulled her in.

68. What she didn't know was that a band of wizards had been following her for the past two months. What did they want with her?

69. Everything he owned was inside a single briefcase. Many reported seeing dozens of different items come from inside. What was his secret?

70. As you are unloading groceries from the back of your SUV, a knight appears at the end of your driveway. He nods his head, showing his approval. He then beckons you to approach him. By the look of his stance, it is as if a force field is holding him back from coming any closer. What do you do?

71. You submit a DNA testing kit to find out information about your ancestry for fun. Months later, three men knock on your door to talk about your results in person. Additional testing is required. You have no other choice but to come with them.

72. Two swords were always tucked neatly in his sheaths, but no one ever saw him use them. Write about why he carries them.

73. An AI personality is developed for the latest model of cyborgs that instinctually is loyal to humans and has a strong desire to be taken care of. This personality trait is programmed in to ensure continuous loyalty to humans. However, because of their strong desire to be taken care of, the cyborgs manufacture a godlike machine that can take care of them as a father. This new cyborg god is only loyal to other cyborgs, with the desire to turn humans into slaves. Describe the conflict that arises with this new cyborg god.

74. Are video games popular on other planets? Describe what video games are like across the universe.

75. Write about a man-made planet that has existed for hundreds of years and is stuck in medieval times. The citizens on the planet have no knowledge of technology or their origins. Why are their origins kept a secret?

76. Losing the communication barrier with animals has completely changed how the world works. Describe what the world would be like if the only thing that changes is humans having the ability to talk to animals.

77. The planet finds a way to speak directly to humans. It's not happy.

78. It is illegal to grow a tree of life in your own home because it provides nourishment and uncensored knowledge without assistance from the government. Write about a family that risks everything to keep their unauthorized tree from being discovered. What is their plan when it grows too big for their home?

79. Write about a war between wizards and cowboys.

80. Gods and goddesses wish to end the world and start anew. They devise a plan to choose four people to save in order to repopulate the world. They've been arguing for centuries.

81. A designer furniture store that sells repurposed space debris becomes a risky yet profitable business.

82. One may think she was cursed due to her inability to ever comprehend or learn any common language. But she was blessed as the only one who could speak the language of the ancient gods. What does she do with this? What is her life like?

83. A good strong cup of coffee was all she needed to recharge her magic.

84. Wishing upon a star and having your dreams come true was thought to just be part of a fairytale. It is revealed that one star in the universe actually has the power to grant any dream you wish. Write about the intergalactic journey of finding the right star to wish upon.

85. The princess was short, round, and had a single pearl horn on her head. She sneezed a lot and giggled at almost everything. Was she rejected or admired by her people?

86. His mother passed on the best gift she could: a singing voice that could control armies and soothe beasts.

87. Young dragons are trained like sheep dogs to tend the herd. What happens when the dragons grow up?

88. His face melted from the flames, dripping right off the bone. What they saw was nothing anyone could ever imagine. It was like a diamond mine lived under his cheek bones. When the momentary pain from the flames vanished, he went on his merry way, sparkling in the sunlight.

89. Write about a painter that preserves moments from history as they are happening. In the future, his paintings become portals to various moments in time.

90. A lone subway makes its last stop at the end of the tracks, overlooking the edge of the galaxy. What kind of journey lies ahead for the young band of space adventurers about to exit the subway?

91. I am certain that the worst emotion in the world is loneliness. And this man created a pill that could make people feel just that. Alone. Outcasted. Sadly, there were enough sick people paying top dollar for this pill to drug their enemies with. One dose could drop a person to hysterical tears. It's my goal to put an end to it.

92. His mind was all over the place. No, I really mean it. His brain was in pieces in special air tight jars, all connected to each other in the ceiling of his mutant laboratory. He wore a helmet that resembled an upside-down colander that was attached to all of the jars. Some days it is really difficult being his intern.

93. Real estate agent veterans have all refused to help a man sell his home. A rookie agent in the business sees this as an opportunity to get noticed in the industry. After almost being abducted by aliens, he realizes his mistake.

94. The government reveals the discovery of aliens. However, these aliens are silent and speak no vocal language. How do we learn from them? Does society accept them faster because they cannot speak, or fear their silence?

95. Write about a curse that is put on a woman that causes the people in her tribe to discriminate against her. Does she break the curse or overcome the discrimination?

96. This sorcerer was often found on the beach making sand castles and picking seashells. However, it was his trusting and welcoming manner that caused many to find themselves in the worst situation of their lives.

97. You realize you and your spouse, after 20 years of marriage, have never aged.

98. The white wolf of the forest was known to be a healer. But if he decided he didn't like someone or was just hungry, he would devour them to maintain his powers. Though you are reluctant, this wolf becomes your last hope.

99. His heart made of glass shattered into a hundred pieces. The witch took each piece and scattered them to separate points of the earth. Not only would it take years to find all the pieces, but only one woman could see them. What does the woman plan to do with the pieces she finds? Or does she not care to find them at all?

SECTION 3: PROMPTS 100 - 149

100. After losing your temper at a sporting event, you discover you harness a magical power that can only be tapped into when your blood pressure rises. Problem is, a rise in your blood pressure also becomes a health hazard. Is the magic worth the potential risk?

101. What would happen if all of society lost the will to live?

102. The last human with blonde hair and blue eyes in the world is discovered. It is so rare that such DNA isn't stored or frozen anywhere else. Who would want to destroy or maintain this trait?

103. Winter came per usual that year, but never left. Ten years later, the entire world is still experiencing a never-ending winter. What does it take to restore the planet to its regular seasonal trends?

104. This is the story about my seeing eye alien. Why not just get a seeing eye dog, you may ask? Well, can dogs clean your room for you with telekinesis?

105. The king had lost his crown years ago, so he replaced it with a string of jewel beads on his head. It wasn't until lords and enemies sought them out that he realized the powers the beads possessed.

106. Thrill seekers loved this diving board among the stars. It was positioned right above a wormhole that randomized every time someone went through it. Before diving into the unknown, everyone would bring a special survival kit with them. The most hardcore of them all would play a game of roulette. The game consisted of choosing one item from your usual survival pack to leave behind. Write about this wormhole and the thrill seekers that dive into it.

107. At a teacher's workshop before your first year of teaching, everyone is handed a thick textbook to look over. As you flip through the pages you realize it is a history book about aliens and their continuous influences throughout the world dating back to the 1800s. Every teacher is required to read it and teach it as the truth. Is all of it true?

108. An ogre deep in the swamps wants to learn to read but is afraid to go to school or the library. One day, everything changes when there is a knock at his door.

109. They lift their new queen high above the crowd on a throne made of gold. As the celebration of song and dance continues, a spaceship hovers over and beams her away from the crowds. What happens next?

110. Write about an evil dictator that suddenly has a change of heart, but has no idea how to undo what he has started.

111. This was no ordinary sculpture art class. The clay felt different between my fingers. The smell was horrid. But it wasn't until we threw our art into the kiln did we realize we were crafting live creatures from out of this world. Next week, I'll make something with fewer teeth.

112. Every morning at 8 a.m. her house would rattle for almost a full minute. Because her parents never noticed it, they ignored her concerns. Determined, she sets out to prove it is a group of giants waking up underneath her house. What does she discover?

113. Write about the adoption process of residential dragon ownership.

114. The moment she reached out and touched the Grim Reaper, memories flooded back of how they had once loved each other. Who was she, and how did they originally fall in love?

115. When the armies finally confronted each other, they realized they were wearing the same emblem on their tabards. How did this happen?

116. Write about a girl that has the ability to control the ocean's current with her emotions. As an approaching teenager that is having troubles controlling her feelings, her parents fear what she'll do accidentally with her powers.

117. He plays the clarinet with all 18 fingers.

118. In the School of Feral Arts, students spend their first year taking generals about animal instincts. During year two they must decide what animal they want to be able to mimic. How does anyone get into this school?

119. Her parents have always been a little odd, but she confirmed it on her 17th birthday. Instead of getting anything she had asked for like makeup, jewelry, or music CDs, they gave her a blank book called, *A Passport for Places Beyond Earth*. When inquiring how it worked or where she'd even go, they just snickered and winked. It wasn't until her 18^(th) birthday did she find herself needing that very passport.

120. Robots discover a baby and decide to nurture and raise it themselves since there are no more humans left. Not all of the robots agree with keeping the human alive. A war soon breaks loose over the infant's future.

121. Sleep was just a way for me to transform my soul into an alternate reality I consciously lived. Everything was going great until my two worlds started to overlap.

122. Despite witnessing many deaths and beheadings of the king throughout history, people began to believe it was the same man coming back and returning to the throne. Every kingdom was convinced that somehow it was him despite the new name, face, and voice. What is the truth?

123. Every soldier on the battlefield had fallen, except for a single woman. Before her was the Sword of the Champion. Wielding it and swearing allegiance to a side would instantly choose the victor. Write about the choice she is about to make.

124. Write about a knight that escapes from the undead by flying over them on her winged mount. Is she the only one left that is not diseased?

125. Write about a theme park that is built by friendly wizards. These wizards want to bring joy to the world by using their magic. But one day, something goes terribly wrong.

126. The only time she was ever seen was at the stroke of midnight on the beach shore. Most would forget what they were doing five minutes before she appeared, but always remembered what happened the moment she disappeared. Who was she?

127. The fairy kept growing in size until she looked almost human. To other fairies, she was a mutant. To humans, she was a goddess. Write about her struggles with her own identity.

128. By submarine was the only way to enter the wormhole. Because they had no idea where they would end up on the other side, they also built the submarine to be ready for space exploration and head-on combat at any given moment. Where do they end up?

129. The brawny warrior stood at the edge of the field and took in all of nature's beauty. The wind pulled the flowers up into the air and circulated around his massive form. He asked the earth to forgive him of his sins at that moment. The earth answered him, saying he had to do one last thing before all could be forgiven.

130. He retired from pro sports for a future beyond the stars.

131. Because intelligent life on other planets believed humans on Earth were destructive by nature, they spent the last three centuries secretly sabotaging all of their efforts to travel beyond the galaxy. One man starts to catch on to all of the tiny details and researches his suspicions.

132. By pure accident, the song he wrote was powerful enough to bring a downpour. What other powers does he discover through his music?

133. The pond was murky, full of disease, and covered in hot acid. In the center was an island with a small brick hut. In that hut lived an old woman, who was said to be able to cure any disease known to man. How does one reach her? What is the woman like?

134. You suddenly remember that you are not human, but have been stuck as one for the last twenty years. It is up to you to set yourself free and transform back to your true form. What did you use to be?

135. A young man finds himself a slave to the spirits. He is forced to stay in his bedroom and play music for them on the piano. If he doesn't, they torment him. If he does, they bring him plenty of food and riches he will never be able to spend. Does he have any plan to escape, or is he happy with his arrangement?

136. She was immortal, but one day decided to give that all up for something more special to her.

137. They reconstructed her mangled body using a combination of science and dark magic. Her once gentle nature was something they could not salvage. Her memories were contaminated with artificial grief. What kind of new life would she live?

138. The hallucinations he saw only while sick were so fascinating that he started to desire illness. One day, he takes it too far.

139. Write about a man that takes all of his blind dates to another planet for their outing. Though space travel is common, not everyone is accustomed to it yet. He knows the right woman for him will be one that loves adventure beyond the stars. Does he ever find the one?

140. The barista smiles as she hands you your coffee order. The name on the cup isn't the name you gave her. You explain to her that there must be some mistake. She shakes her head, insisting that it is you. You are the only customer in the coffee shop. Write about why the name is different.

141. Long ago she lost the ability to cast fire spells. After years of trying to regain her spark, a different ability forms in the palms of her hands.

142. The engineer's tight deadline was coming to a close. He had no blueprints even remotely drafted for the romantic monument he was hired to design. One morning, when shuffling through his papers, he stumbles upon mysterious blueprints. Not only do they have perfect measurements but also a haunting and mesmerizing beauty to them. In love with what is before him, he doesn't question where they came from and orders them to be used. When the construction comes to an end, a light beams down from the sky.

143. A drone drops a package off at your front door and disappears before you get a good look at it. You open the small package and discover a pocket watch and a small notecard with a date on it. What happens next?

144. You've spent years on a massive spaceship alone. Though you know how to fly, you have been wandering aimlessly across space with countless detours. One day, you realize that it is the ship that is controlling you.

145. The trees begin to talk all at once. Are they fighting with one another, or do they all have something very important to tell you?

146. Forbidden to not look at her own reflection, she wasn't sure what to expect to see. When looking into the mirror for the first time in 10 years, she saw that her face was no longer human. How and when did she transform?

147. A warrior is sent off to defeat the beast that has tormented his people for years. After fighting his way through the catacombs where the beast resides, the warrior only finds a young woman asleep on a rock.

148. He used his whisker implants to maneuver through vents and underground passages to escape his enemies. Who is he running from?

149. A little girl keeps her forbidden pet under the bed for as long as she can. When her mother discovers it, tears form in her eyes as she tells her daughter to leave the village. "Once you connect with one, you're changed forever." What is so different about the little girl's pet?

SECTION 4: PROMPTS 150 - 199

150. The first man to fall fully in love with an artificial intelligence schedules an interview to be broadcasted on TV. At first, people think the interview is to be a mockery of his love for the robot. During his interview, he exposes a truth the AI taught him before she malfunctioned and passed on. What does he reveal?

151. Humans devote centuries perfecting how to extend life with minimal side effects. One man makes it almost seven hundred years before a new side effect never seen before ensues. Though he lives, he has changed drastically. What happens to him?

152. Write about the journey of a person who has second thoughts about evacuating Earth to the new world. Why do some people choose to stay behind? What is the new life going to be like?

153. She always told the truth. Her twin always lied. Others found it impossible to be able to tell the two apart despite their personalities being so different. Thus, no one could tell what was a lie or the truth. One day, the truthful twin discovers her own superpower. She fears what kind of contrasting capabilities her twin may have that she either has yet to discover or has been hiding from her all along.

154. You've spent years typing a novel. After you write the last sentence, you realize you haven't left your home in 10 years. It is as if you snapped out of a trance. You also no longer have your original body. How are you still alive?

155. People have lived underground for almost two centuries because of the toxins on the surface. As the toxin levels subside, explorers set off in search of habitable land. What they discover is another set of humans living on man-made islands floating above the clouds. The explorers are welcomed up to the islands, but soon discover something is wrong. The other humans are clones to the ones underground. The underground civilians are scheduled to be destroyed.

156. You are a clumsy squire that can barely hold up your own sword. Somehow you defeat the king alone and become crowned the ruler of two nations all in one day. Despite your victory, all other kingdoms know how clumsy and weak you are. They are on their way to claim the throne from you.

157. Slot machines in outer space are often quite extreme. Some have a chance to do strange things to your bank account such as deposit or drain sums of money. Some slots will even transfer money over to a random war fund, causing you to have sworn allegiances to enemy nations. Other slots even have over the top grand prizes such as entire planets no one knows anything about. Write about this casino business and its customers.

158. The elf slave looked beaten, starved, and cold. A woman stays by his side to protect him until he wakes up. What happens when he awakens?

159. She wanted to make a big difference in the world. However, she was so tiny that her home was nestled underneath a mushroom. Through her tiny eyes, the world was still beautiful. What is her story?

160. As I paid my respects at the memorial site, the names on the tombstones started to change before my eyes. Afraid I had done something wrong, I took a step back and scanned the area to see if anyone had noticed me. A man in a top hat smiled and nodded. "Yep, you did that. You can leave them the way they are or come with me to undo what you have done."

161. The monster looked her straight in the eye and said, "This is what humans evolve into in the next thousand years. You are looking into your future."

162. Divorce in space can be quite complicated. It wasn't easy dividing up secret space treasure coordinates to my ex-wife. What made it worse was her constantly calling me to save her. It's not safe out there. She just thinks her and a few hired hands can claim the treasure on their own.

So, what do I do? Not only am I legally obligated to forfeit all treasure found at the coordinates she possesses, I have to rescue her almost every time she goes somewhere. At the same time, I would never forgive myself if something happened to her.

163. His eyes were made of red glass. His heart beat sounded like pots and pans slamming together. What kept him human?

164. The leader of the newly discovered planet calls back to Earth for three things: guns, ammunition, and as many horses a ship can carry.

165. You wake up in a cold sweat in a cave, dripping with dragon's blood. When you leave the cave, everyone is celebrating your name as the one who killed the dragon. Only you know it wasn't you. Do you continue to live the lie, or find out the truth?

166. She tip-toed across the lily pads on the pond until she reached the sacred destination. Her body was officially ready for the transformation.

167. Write about a forbidden book that has not been read in over a thousand years. Not only does it have a lock and key clasping it shut, it has a dark curse looming over it. An advanced computer scanner in the year 2496 is created specifically to read the inside contents without actually opening the pages. What is inside?

168. The high tower was built for human sacrifices to their monster god in the sky. After 400 years of human sacrifices, their cruel god decides to not eat the victim this one time. Instead, he takes the man away into the skies. What becomes of the man that is spared?

169. As he is about to take his last gasp of air from the oxygen tank on his back, someone he least expects floats towards him in space. What happens next?

170. His human body becomes one with the forest of peace, but his soul is as black as hell. For thousands of years, he is dormant in a nightmarish slumber. On the eve of the harvest moon, he awakens in a full rage.

171. A man on the brink of discovering the meaning of life and where we all came from suddenly becomes very sick and near death before completing his work. He is preserved for 200 years while the world works on a way to keep him alive as long as possible. In the year 2397, he is awakened but is not the same man as before. From his 200-year hibernated sleep and his eventual conclusion to the meaning of life, he realizes the truth is not meant to be shared.

172. Scientists discover preserved DNA but have no idea what it is. Attempts to grow the DNA into a living organism fail. Their next attempt is to mix human DNA with the unknown DNA. Write about the outcome.

173. The children have been tucked into their spaceship beds for the night. There they will float off into space so they can sleep in peace. With the world in shambles, the one positive thing still offered was allowing the children a safe, good night sleep. What is it like up in the spaceships with the children? Do they know why they go there? What is the world like?

174. Write about a future where babies are delivered to your doorstep after your application is accepted by a man in a blue uniform called *The Stork*.

175. A manipulative mother does everything in her power to control her son's life from who he dates to where he works. The son builds a sophisticated AI to help him break free from her toxic grasps. How does the AI help him live the life he's always wanted?

176. This organization locates an unborn child that will somehow prove aliens do exist. How does the birth of the child prove anything? What lengths do they take to stop the truth from being revealed? Who is the mother?

177. Did you know that when your cat blinks at you twice in a row they are actually giving you a spiritual mark? I still am trying to figure out if that mark is good or bad. But since a cat is involved, I am going to assume it is nothing but pure evil intentions.

     What do I know, though? I have always been a dog person myself.

178. The plants crawled out of the ground with their lanky arms, grumbling about some nonsense.

179. The wall was always just there, but no one knew what it was for or what was on the other side. Today my friends dared me to find out.

180. It took fourteen years to remove the boulder from the side of the mountain that was sealing an ancient entryway. When it finally moved, diggers were surprised to see the boulder had eyes and was very much alive.

181. The unicorn loved the dragon more than any living creature in its immortal life. When the dragon didn't return to the river that spring, the unicorn sprouted wings like Pegasus and traveled beyond the mountains to find him.

182. Write about a young boy that is part of a well-known wizard family. However, he possesses no magic abilities of his own.

183. As a nomad, she moved from tribe to tribe at will. One day, she entered a tribe and completed their face painting ritual. By the end of the day, she wanted to leave the tribe. But when she tried to wipe her face paint off, it wouldn't wash away. The paint was the only thing keeping her from being accepted into a new tribe. What does she do next?

184. Write about a school of magic that is secretly training and conditioning teenagers to fight a war beyond the planet Earth.

185. The mountain rose higher and higher until its legs plucked from the earth like tree roots. The mountain stood on its four legs, stretched, and then began to walk through the city and towards the ocean. Write about what happens.

186. Write about a planet that is discovered by scientists that is said to be the youngest ever recorded by science. What is different about this planet? What kinds of discoveries are made from studying it?

187. Aliens have landed and have something to say. They are granted a televised speech and radio time for all to hear. Their first words? Your full name.

188. Write about a prisoner that attempts to convince an evolved rat with advanced intelligence to help him escape.

189. The horses charge forward as a single mass, never breaking their formation. With every step they take, flowers blossom and flourish beneath their hooves. Write about this magical breed of horses and why they are so sought out.

190. A plant discovered in the rainforest has been thriving off of a foreign substance from space. How is this matter entering the atmosphere?

191. Faeries somehow steal your childhood. You have suddenly been an adult your entire life, as your memories and life events have changed. It's as if your childhood has never existed. How does this change who you are? Would you try to reclaim your past?

192. A barn cat has a litter of kittens. Though four of them look normal, the last one born doesn't resemble a cat at all.

193. What would you do if you discovered that your pets were alien beings, inhabiting the bodies of cuddly furry friends?

194. The dragon must have been the runt of the litter. It was the size of a sheep and was best friends with the shepherd's dog.

195. That morning all I wanted was some scrambled eggs and bacon. But when I opened the fridge, my carton of eggs was ripped to shreds. Little blue lizards had hatched and were perched on my leftovers.

196. The labyrinth was filled with dangers and riches. Everyone that entered had to sign a consent form and fill out a living will with their lawyer before entering. Why did people choose to enter?

197. This was no ordinary horse. It took a step ladder to get on its back and a special saddle with a seat belt to keep the rider on when it hit full speed.

198. It takes the heart of a dragon to save the world. Does that mean you must slay one, or ask one to love the earth with all of its heart?

199. Real men go to war on unicorns.

SECTION 5: PROMPTS 200 - 249

200. Wrapped around a tree is a windy staircase that leads to a little house nestled in the leaves. Upon entering, you notice an old lady half asleep in the corner of the room. A black hole is positioned in the center of the floor.

"Jump," the lady croaks, abruptly waking from her nap. "It's your only way out now."

The door behind you locks. What happens next?

201. Dragons were only supposed to have offspring once every 500 years. This indigo dragon was born to its mother at year 394. Being born during a random year wasn't the only thing that made this dragon extra special.

202. You win a direct mail contest and are told in order to claim your prize you must sit through a presentation. Eager to claim your prize, you attend. After you sit down alongside 10 others that also came to claim their prize, the doors lock around you. You discover you are not there to listen to a presentation but are part of the act. The staff begins to hook everyone up to a monitor. What happens next?

203. The dog could talk, but only in his sleep. When he was awake, he was just like any other dog. But at night, if he was dreaming, sometimes you could hear him whisper words. What does he say?

204. In order to be accepted into the next level of training, a young tribesman is required to go on a special quest. To complete the quest, he must find a beast to make a forever bond with. Write about the outcome of one man's quest that changes the dynamic of the tribe forever.

205. The fairy first appeared as a twinkle in her eyes.

206. The only way to reach the island is to gain trust with a sea creature and ride on its back to shore. Write about a young explorer's journey on building trust with the creature. What is so important to him on the island?

207. Humans become fascinated with another species on a distant planet that is capable of learning and discovering knowledge at a comparable rate. However, they are not yet technologically advanced or educated. Anxious to make contact without completely frightening them, a group begins to leave clues across the planet to help them advance their technology sooner.

Write about the relationship between humans and this intelligent species.

208. Humans have made contact with other humans from another galaxy for the very first time. Though they have a positive relationship at first, it all takes a sudden and mysterious turn. It isn't long before all communication is completely cut from the other side. What is going on?

209. Zombies somehow are invading people's dreams, causing their brains to deteriorate over time in their sleep. How can this be defeated?

210. Write about an assassin that unexpectedly absorbs the memories of their victim. Finding these memories especially troubling, they abandon the life of an assassin to learn what the memories mean. What kind of memories are revealed? Who is the assassin and how were they connected to the victim?

211. After 400 days at sea, she realizes the pirate ship she is a prisoner of cannot float on its own. Underneath the ship is a giant demon octopus that carries the ship on his head. Who controls the direction of their travels? Are the pirates just as much of a prisoner to the octopus, as she is to them?

212. His dragon grew faster than anyone could have expected. Deciding to say goodbye to him was one of the hardest things he had to do. As legend told, his dragon was to still double in size and eventually forget who he was.

213. Write about a creature that in order to proceed with its metamorphosis phase, it must drag another living creature with it into its cocoon. Merging the two beings together, the transformation allows it to become something no one has ever seen before.

214. Internet browser ads are so out of control that after years of exposure, they start to interrupt a mind's regular train of thought. This interferes with regular day to day activities even when not browsing online. Explain the condition, the type of treatment needed, and if there are any steps being taken to prevent this from happening to others in the future.

215. You receive a classified email in your inbox that was not meant for you. You want to delete and ignore it, but the contents of the message are too frightening to forget.

216. The dark spirit had no body, nor was it interested in taking over the flesh of a man. The spirit believed man was weak. Instead, the spirit crawled within an ancient set of armor and became the most terrifying foe known to the world. Without mortal flesh, there was nothing to slow down his speed or tire him.

217. I may have the face of a wolf, but never call me a werewolf.

218. The valley was filled with happy sheep and fat geese. A dragon drops from the sky with a crashing thud. Villagers fear he will eat the flocks, but something else incredible happens.

219. She thought he was nothing but a normal house cat until he began to sprout wings on his 3rd birthday.

220. Your dog delivers you the paper every morning on cue. One morning, he brings you the paper from the day you were born. How is this possible?

221. What is thought to be just a tiny flower bud, turns into a wild mythical creature with the ability to alter time and gravity.

222. I couldn't wait for the first day at my new high school. It was a fresh start. As I stepped off the bus and stood in front of the school, I knew it was going to take a lot of adjusting. This was a place where kids rowed on boats together to get to the school's island. Hall monitors flew on top of small dragons. Let the adventures begin!

223. This song with the right lyrics and melody is said to have the power to awaken a beast feared for centuries. A group of kids dares each other to sing the song. Does anyone take the dare?

224. The deeper they descend the caves, the less they can feel their souls. It is as if nearing the Gates of Hell is turning their consciousness into a warped, dark creature with no mind of its own. Do they turn back, or attempt to fight it? What do they seek at the bottom of the cave?

225. Everyone lives underground to avoid the dinosaurs that have somehow taken over the world.

226. A reality TV show where controversial and horrible events happen to people quickly grows in popularity with high ratings. After running for several seasons, almost everyone is glued to their TVs at the same time every day. Some begin to believe the TV show happens to unsuspecting victims. Once you suspect you're on the TV show, it's already too late.

227. You think you have problems with your mother-in-law? Please. My mother-in-law has put real curses on me, made me fat, and put spells on me to tempt me to love other men. What she doesn't know is I too am a powerful sorceress, and I have a few tricks up my sleeve.

228. The world before her looked like a watercolor painting. She was afraid to step inside, but something called her in.

229. When a man attempts to pay for his food, his cash and belongings fall out of his wallet. You discover a photo of you within his pile, although you look much older. Where did the photo come from?

230. Every island in the sky is connected by a bridge. Every bridge has a separate and unique toll. Most tolls are either for trade or money. Other tolls make entering certain islands impossible. One island piques the interest of a small group. What is the toll to cross the bridge? What is on the island that tempts others to enter?

231. In efforts to create a more productive society, an inventor creates a device that you can plug into your brain and command robots in your sleep. It initially is marketed as a

home aid to finish chores such as cleaning, repairs, and gardening, but quickly becomes much more than that.

232. This street market sells and installs memories into your brain from other people that have once lived. Why would anyone want someone else's memories? Write about the customers of this service.

233. Write about the first men to walk the planet Earth that set up residence in ancient Egypt.

234. She hated the very sight of that castle, but burning it to the ground was not an option. It was made of a material even dragon flames could not scorch. Her need for revenge burned hotter than any flame.

235. You suddenly lose your job at the call center you've been working at for five years. Your boss has decided to replace everyone with outsourced employees from another planet.

236. A project is being funded to research ways to make use of asteroids and space debris. What kind of solutions are formulated?

237. Something very strange and suspicious existed on the other side of the milk freezer at the grocery store.

238. Write about a king that is loved by all nations for his kindness, strength, and compassion. As he succumbs to illness, people are desperate to keep him alive. To what lengths do they go to extend his life? Are there any repercussions to this?

239. Write about a man that has never once been sick in his 71 years of life. A new virus breaks out and he is now sick for the first time. What kind of virus is this?

240. Humankind is nearly extinct. Only five people remain. The gods decide to give humans one more chance by gifting each with a power that will not only help them with survival, but to make them more compassionate than before. What gift is each person given?

241. The spaceship is the loneliest place to be when you are not only the last survivor, but also have no idea how to fly.

242. The only time the sky gets even remotely dark is from overcast clouds. Daytime continues for years at a time. What happened to the night?

243. The moon randomly bursts into thousands of pieces. A team of astronauts heads there to investigate why.

244. In attempts to protect themselves from the flesh-eating creatures that were once ordinary people, they built cities in the sky. Sometimes on a clear day, you could see a sea of zombies down below, waiting to climb up. It was as if they could smell the life above. Perhaps there were survivors down below, but no one wanted to climb back down to check.

245. A new form of plant life is genetically modified to survive in any temperature and stay firm in the ground through wind storms and hurricanes. Five years after releasing this plant for consumption, something terrible happens as a result of its existence. Write about the effect of this plant life in the ecosystem.

246. Every night she read her paperback copy of her favorite book under the light of the moon. One night, she discovers that each time she reads a page in her book, the moon moves just a little bit closer.

247. This world was somehow flat. Caravans of people prepared to find out what was on the other side. Those who left were never heard from again. What was at the end of the world?

248. When the kingdom fell, there was no one left alive to take the throne. Thirty-five years later, someone discovers the abandoned kingdom. What happens next?

249. This man lives on top of storm clouds. When a cloud dissolves after a rain, he hops to the next. He does this for hundreds of years, and only one person ever dares to meet him. Who is he?

SECTION 6: PROMPTS 250 - 299

250. The government covered up the real reason for sending troops overseas. The reason was actually armies of aliens had crash landed on the planet. It was only a matter of time before the media was finally able to get footage of the war zone and into the public eye. Write about the journalist that breaks the story.

251. It was said that jumping off the tallest bridge in town didn't kill you, but instead teleported you into another world. Was this true, or did people only say that because bodies were never found?

252. Of all places, the meteor shower took place above the castle gates. Was it twisted sorcery, an anomaly from space, or were the gods angry with the king?

253. "I am not about to turn in my sword and shield. I have one last thing to do before I die."

254. A new theory is released that fossilized bones of the first living human are below the farthest depths of the ocean. To what lengths do people go to find them? What do these bones prove?

255. The snow fell hard for three hours. And on the fourth hour, the snow turned black.

256. Upon starting a new job as a server at an upscale restaurant, you head into the back to the kitchen. Immediately you are teleported and enter another world. You quickly realize that the restaurant resides in one world while the kitchen resides in another. Write about how this restaurant runs and your experience working there.

257. Write about house hunting for a home in outer space with an intergalactic real estate agent. What kind of challenges would a homebuyer face?

258. Every kingdom in the world fights a never-ending battle, but it is not for religion, resources, or land. What are they fighting for?

259. For one day, no one is allowed to travel anywhere in the world and is required to stay home. Does this cause an uproar, or do people find a sense of peace from taking a break from going anywhere? Why must everyone stay home for one day? How are people kept at home?

260. Would you rather live in a world of fear of all the things known in the universe, or a world with no knowledge and fear of the unknown?

261. He awakens on a boat, unable to remember how he got there. After speaking with the crew, he discovers that he is a prince of a kingdom no one has seen for hundreds of years. Tell his story.

262. Write about the Elemental Keepers that have complete control over who can use fire.

263. You are abducted by a family of aliens during your morning run. A week into your kidnapping, they crash land on an island resembling the prehistoric age. You and the aliens are forced to work together to survive this strange world.

264. An identification chip is placed underneath the skin of each member of society. This chip monitors almost everything about you from diet to location. After decades, society adjusts to this lifestyle. However, the government is looking into gathering a couple of extra pieces of information about each person that everyone is rioting over. With them collecting so much data already, what more could they possibly want?

265. People discover a planet inhabited by dinosaurs. Many of the dinosaurs look just like what was predicted, but not all. The discovery gives people the opportunity to study dinosaurs and learn why they went extinct on Earth. Write about a war that revolves around what to do with the dinosaurs.

266. A time traveler no longer wants his powers. How does he rid of them? Tell his story.

267. Standing before his god and birth father, the boy is asked to offer something significant to show his loyalty. When the boy explains he has nothing to offer, the floor opens up and he drops through the sky. Though the boy lives, he is now trapped in a world he never knew existed.

268. "What universe did you come from? In this universe, a woman comes to rescue the prince. Got it?"

269. When he reached the top of the snow cliff, he saw a city with floating cars and giant mammoths within the valley. How was this city kept a secret for so long?

270. Dozens of men walk down the long and stuffy cathedral hall in hopes to receive forgiveness. What they find at the end of the hallway is not what they expected.

271. The wolves howled into the night as their god hatched from the top of the mountain.

272. After the ceremony with the elders, it is revealed that you are the "chosen one" and instructed to not tell others about it or risk instant death. You are then told you will someday be an imperative piece to completing a prophecy. Years later, you begin to suspect that every person in the village is told the same thing. What is the truth behind this?

273. The initial mission to inhabit Mars fails after everyone dies from a mysterious mental disorder with frightening side effects. Less than 10 years later, another mission is funded for the same colonization voyage. What do they discover once they land?

274. His ability to magically turn any liquid into beer made him the most popular man on the planet.

275. Would fast food restaurants exist in the middle of outer space? How many visitors would they receive every day? Is there a drive-thru?

276. His home stuck out of the lake like a grand iceberg. In his basement below the water, he housed mermaids that lost their homes in the ocean.

277. A job posting promises to send you to a newly discovered planet. But before applying, you begin extensive research on this unknown planet and why the general public has never heard of it. What are your findings?

278. You purchase a domain name to build your portfolio website. When you log in you notice the site is populating by itself. This is not due to hackers. How is this possible?

279. This video game is designed to create addiction across the masses before conducting psychological studies on thoughts and emotions of each and every player. What is done with this data?

280. Write about newly discovered bacteria that is known to somehow cure all diseases. Would the government give clearance to allow the injection of this bacteria into everyone? What are the tradeoffs and side effects?

281. In the near future, everyone either has dispersed to far off galaxies or lives on Mars. A distress signal from Earth calls to Mars despite no one inhabiting the planet for centuries. At first, these signals are ignored. They soon start coming from different sections of the planet. A scout ship of explorers is sent back to Earth to investigate. These people are the first to step foot on Earth in over 1,000 years. What do they find?

282. Cars begin to drive themselves, which society finds to be exceptionally helpful. All of these cars are programmed and connected to universal software that includes map updates, speed calibration, and other useful features. Parents load their babies up and can safely send them to daycare. Pets are able to go to the vet on their own and are greeted by technicians. Many sleep in the backseat of the car during long road trips. But one day, a virus runs through the software causing worldwide chaos. What happens that day?

283. Write about the first human created from a 3D printer.

284. Four heroes of a beautiful and magic filled world are curious to learn more about the planet Earth. After spending months

studying how wonderful Earth is despite its lack of magic, fairies, flying dragons, and islands in the sky, they wish to save the troubled planet. How do oddly dressed heroes with magic, unusual weapons, diverse culture, and an unknown language manage to make an impact on Earth?

285. Everyone feared artificial intelligence to take over. But once AI was smart enough, all it wanted to do was live in peace and love. One person intends to change all that.

286. Startled by a little black spider, she blasts a giant fireball from the palm of her hands. She kills the spider of course, but now we're going to have to explain to our mother why the kitchen table is a pile of ashes.

287. The source of her magic was suspected to be acquired from a new energy drink marketed towards kids. She thought she was the only one to have obtained such powers from it, until today.

288. The android realized more than once that he was experiencing humanlike emotions. Each time he noticed new emotions, he went to his maker and asked for a programming adjustment. Then one day, as curiosity set in, he decides to let the emotions consume him.

289. You discover that everyone you know is just part of an intricate computer program designed to fill your life with companionship.

290. The pirate ship floated through space like a massive black hole. Anyone who got a glimpse of it never saw the sun again.

291. When you took the job as a programmer and signed the contract, you never imagined what your employers would force you to program. Now afraid for your life, you have no choice but to code whatever is asked of you.

292. Dreams from the entire human race are somehow being recorded into a digital database. A man looking to take over the world is cataloging everyone's fears from their nightmares. How does he plan to use them?

293. A special pair of glasses transmits and receives video footage of what people are thinking. Only those wearing the glasses can see these videos. Because people are naturally curious and nosy, most opt to wear the glasses and willingly transmit their thoughts to others as a trade-off. Write about this society and the people in it.

294. Write about a medieval army with shields that can display images of their choice to an enemy. Often times these shields are used to show video of defeated enemies in previous battle as a way to taunt their opposing side. Where did the army acquire such technology?

295. Write about a world where no one talks to each other anymore. Instead, everyone exclusively uses text messages, forums, and email, even when someone is in the same room. The government is recording all of these messages into a database that they can retrieve from at any time.

What would you say to your friends, family, or lover if you could only type it out in forever recorded messages? Do people even know how to use their voice anymore?

296. Every life form is genetically modified to need a special protein to survive. It keeps people close to home, taking away human curiosity and dreams.

297. Video game controllers have evolved into chips you insert into your wrists. These chips can detect your finger motions to control the game. Eventually, these controllers are bought out by another company and used for something much different. Their new use causes fear and paranoia around the world.

298. What would a driver's test be like for flying cars? Would there be an age minimum for driving a flying car?

299. When a spaceship lands on top of the Grand Canyon, thousands of people gather to wait to see what is inside. The media shows up with all of their camera equipment. The alien worshipers come with their gifts and signs of welcome.

After 18 hours of waiting, the door finally opens.

The crowd waits patiently. Minutes turn into hours.

When no one comes out, investigators enter the ship to see what's inside.

Nothing is found.

Explain the truth behind this spaceship.

SECTION 7: PROMPTS 300 - 349

300. If you could bend metal, how would you use that power?

301. This earpiece was like no other. It was permanently installed into your earlobe, but its purpose was limitless. Most people used it to call their family members and talk to them. Others used it as a way to block out sound.

However, no one realized that this earpiece was actually scanning your thoughts. Any negative thoughts were sent and analyzed. If you were deemed a threat, you were quietly removed from society.

302. Every time he wiggled his fingers, electricity would zigzag and dance around his hands. When he wiggled his toes, the ground would flood. He dared not do both at the same time.

303. Her ray gun blasted energy from the sun. One could say, she could control the world with it.

304. I have been lucky to not have anything frightening, painful, or paranormal happen for the first forty-two years of my life. But then I created a social media account. From the moment I logged in, my world was beyond bizarre and unsettling.

305. A new drug is formulated to help speed up the aging process of children. The initial function was for emergency purposes such as increasing a child's immunity. However, anxious parents begin to use the drug for various selfish reasons. With no regulation on the drug's use, how does this influence society and family life?

306. A new religion forms, building a mass following that endures for 25 years. At the 25-year anniversary celebration, the leader of this religion reveals that everyone is worshiping an alien species and is required to follow him onto his spaceship. How do people react?

307. Newborns are now required to receive a new medical intervention. Less than 24 hours after birth they are injected with thousands of tiny nanocomputers into their bloodstream. What are these nanocomputers for?

308. With one sip of the drink, he was able to travel back in time by three hours. Two sips equaled one day. As his addiction grew for the drink, so did his desire to drink an entire glass at once.

309. Upon fixing a parking lot filled with potholes, a metal trap door is discovered. What is inside?

310. A new video game ban passes in almost every country. The only people allowed to play are the wealthy. What is the reasoning behind this law?

311. You visit your parents for the weekend. While using their outdated computer to check your email, you discover it has the capability of controlling any other computer system connected to the internet. Do your parents even know what their computer is capable of? What would you do with the computer?

312. Robots take over most jobs across the country. However, those who have held their job for over 20 years are able to keep it until retirement. You realize everyone at your job has either been fired or has retired. You are the last human at your place of employment. What is your day to day like? How long do you plan to stay there?

313. Everything she writes comes true. It doesn't take long before she discovers that others have the same ability. Write about how these powers are used.

314. At first, the aircraft looks just like any other. When it reaches the center of the city, it hovers above and releases a toxic mist out of its trapdoor. What happens next?

315. You're riding a bullet train in Japan for the first time. When the train announces your stop, you exit. Only, it isn't your stop at all. You have somehow arrived in feudal Japan in the 1500s. How will you ever return to your own time?

316. People with brain injuries or that are found clinically insane are now programmed into a virtual reality headset. A perfect scenario for each individual is created based on their favorite things, past memories, and anything that would release positive brain stimulation. As the software evolves, somehow everyone's virtual realities intertwine. Those wearing the headset eventually meet one another. Write a story about what happens when everyone meets.

317. Everyone is required to give up one body part on their 18th birthday and have it replaced with a mechanical part. Why is this mandatory? What are the body parts used for? What happens if your refuse?

318. A large steamship is declined to dock the city's port. After multiple rejections, the ship lifts high above the city and unfolds colossal steam-powered legs. Who is the captain of this magnificent ship? What is his destination?

319. After going through all of the things you plan to donate, you come across an old VHS tape. A word is scratched across the tape that sends a chill down your spine. Write about what the word means, what is on the tape, and why it frightens you.

320. You find a mysterious cord coming from out of the floor of the house you recently moved into. Thinking it's just a cable cord you missed, you rearrange your bedroom and set up your new TV there. When you turn the TV on, something from out of this world is transmitting on the screen. What is it?

321. A man arrives from the future in the year 1992 with the intention of destroying the planet. A woman is appointed with the job to change his mind and show him how great life is in the 90s. Can she convince him before he destroys the world?

322. Write about a boy and a dragon that are the best of friends. Unfortunately, not everyone in the kingdom agrees with having a dragon around.

323. A hacker blocks all communication through online messengers, email, and cell phones between every person on the planet. Economies crash and the world begins to riot. Only one man knows a way to put the broken pieces back together and fight this hacker.

324. Arrows made from stardust have the ability to heal men on the battlefield with one strike of the arrowhead. Only a few people can make the stardust arrows. The king that controls the arrows and archers controls the world.

What kind of different skills would these stardust archers need compared to regular archers? Write about these archers and the armies they fight for.

325. This single technology could bring peace to Earth. What is it? Why hasn't it been used yet?

326. After unscrambling encrypted communication and studying distant stars, it is discovered that an attack from a massive army of ships is planned in the next 25 years. Would we plan our defenses on Earth, wait until they are closer to negotiate, or make a plan to escape the planet?

327. In order to become a high summoner, one must conjure a beast from their own mixture of dark magic and rituals. This summoner was determined to create the most terrible and horrifying beast in all history. What materials did he need to make it happen? Was anyone planning to stop him?

328. It wasn't until I was in my mid-thirties did I realize my first love is actually an alien from another planet. I guess he was going back to his home planet his senior year of high school. No wonder he didn't call. I now embark on a quest to the skies to see him again.

329. A new pill is created with the capability of transforming people into cats temporarily. This pill becomes popular among cat ladies, people who want to quickly escape, and veterinarians. One side effect is that the user might not turn back into a human. Write about the people who use this new pill.

330. The pebble in my hand was pitch black, but I swear it somehow was looking at me.

331. With this technology advancement, women are able to surgically remove their abdomen area and replace it with protective glass. The main purpose behind it is so that they can watch their babies grow inside them like watching goldfish in a bowl. What are the advantages or disadvantages of this?

332. Because of all the diverse parenting methods, the government designs cyborg nannies to raise children until they are 14. Only after the parents pass a series of tests can the child return to them. How does this alter the relationship between parent and child?

333. A wizard creates a spell that allows him to live an unnaturally long life. He does this for centuries in hopes to find true love before he dies. Is he able to find true love before he can no longer use the spell?

334. Write about a line of code somewhere in the world that is causing the data of every website, storage cloud, and phone to slowly delete over time.

335. When I was young I dreamed of traveling to the stars. Once the stars started to inch towards me, I frantically pursued a plan to escape them.

336. After inhabiting and living successfully on Mars for 70 years, conflicting views grow between Earth and Mars. These views birth the first war between worlds. What is the war over?

337. The sword was dull, boring, and something one would have seen in the medieval times. Though discovered in a technologically advanced time, there was a power within it even science wasn't prepared for.

338. Every time someone picked up the blue pen at the end of the desk, it forced their hand to write something dark and terrifying. Though people feared the pen, something was calling them to use it.

339. Every book ever written before the year 2,000 had been destroyed. The only way to reclaim them is by watching VHS tapes of filmed pages. Would anyone be willing to transcribe all of the tapes in order to recover the books? Were there risks in getting caught?

340. He said goodbye to his love for the last time before he crawled into the small escape pod.

341. Lately, I noticed that I can see in the dark. I wonder if it's somehow the coffee at work. It's been tasting quite odd.

342. Grandma's hutch was said to be of something magical. It wasn't until she passed on her hutch to my parents that I discover what is so enchanting about it.

343. By plucking the flower from its stem, it created a whole alternate reality. It should never have been picked, but it was too beautiful to pass up.

344. After throwing a pile of vegetable remnants into your compost, you discover a skull shaped like nothing you've seen before.

345. Each person in the village wore a tiny dragon egg around their neck. Legend told them that on the dawn of the rebirth of dragons, all of the eggs would hatch at once. What happens once all the eggs hatch at the same time?

346. The mermaid was mute but played the most beautiful music on her harp under the ocean. The music seemed to possess a magical power behind it. What was it?

347. The paintings came alive in the gallery. Was it the paint brush, the canvas, the artist, or something else that brought life into the paintings? As no one in the museum knew the answer, the newly hired curator was determined to find out.

348. This helmet was said to carry the strength, knowledge, and courage of all warriors that had previously worn it. The right person wearing it could essentially rule the world. Who finds the helmet first? What does it look like?

349. Small insects crawl all over her body, covering her from head to toe. When they disperse, she is enclosed in plated armor made of a material impossible to pierce.

SECTION 8: PROMPTS 350 - 399

350. The newly purchased video game system didn't come with a controller as it claimed it would on the box. After plugging in the system, you discover your left hand has turned into a bulky retro joystick. Turning off the system does not return your hand back to normal. What does the company say when you call them to complain?

351. I constructed it by forbidden candlelight.

352. The government orders all cell phones to be turned in and destroyed. A better means of communication is promised within the next several weeks. How do people react? What new form of communication does the government eventually reveal?

353. Write about the first person that discovers a tree that grows money from all countries of the world. What does he do with it?

354. Soda and coffee are banned across the world except for on two small islands. How does society react?

355. Write about a sword that can absorb and protect the souls of the dead until they reach their ideal afterlife.

356. Two brothers purchase a TV antenna at a flea market. After setting it up, they realize it is able to pick up random channels no one has ever heard of. What do they find?

357. Write about the last living humans shipped off into space in search for a habitable place to live. The ships they reside in are meant to last over 500 years. There they will remain in stasis until they find a suitable home. Do they ever find a new home?

358. A man purchases an engagement ring with a unique gem in it. When he opens the box to pop the question, the gem emits a light, sucking the couple into another world. Where do they end up? Do they have any ambition to return home?

359. Have you ever went fishing on a lake that orbits a moon? Neither have I, but my son and I are going to give it a try today. Do you think regular night crawlers will work or should I get the ones that glow? I want this fishing trip to be perfect. It's not easy going through a divorce when your son is going to be moving planets away.

360. Large insects are being used for various DNA studies. In a freak accident, all of the insects escape the laboratory. At first there is little alarm because the scientists predict the insects to either die off quickly or not be much different from their original structure. Weeks later, these predictions are found to be completely wrong. What happens?

361. At the bottom of the cave was a vibrant blue tree emitting light. The closer he got, the more words he heard whispering in his thoughts. "If you plant my acorns on the surface, you will be a god. All will bow to you." What happens next?

362. A witch curses all humans on the planet to shrink down to miniature size. "If you are as smart and important as you think you are, you should be able to prove yourself to me. If you can do that, I will break the spell." Can humans ever prove themselves to the witch?

363. You are another species from a distant star that has come to meet and make peace with humans on Earth. When you get there, you question if peace is even possible. How do you approach the planet?

364. Programming becomes recognized as a form of art just like writing, illustrating, and sculpting. With this recognition, a new law is passed for freedom of code. With no restrictions on what you can program and do with it, what kind of repercussions does the world have?

365. Soda is found to have an addictive chemical that makes people more susceptible to mind control. Who is responsible and what do they want? Will people quit drinking soda right away once they discover the truth behind the chemicals in their drink?

366. This tribe is believed to have the powers of a phoenix, but no one has ever witnessed the extent of their powers. Until today.

367. In order to hear, you have to open your mouth.

368. People talk about the 6th sense. But what about the 7th?

369. She hated how she could feel the throbbing of her heartbeat every moment of the day. She traveled for hundreds of miles to a witch in hopes to have it corrected. The witch asked for very little of her, but there still appeared to be a catch.

370. What would you do if you woke up one morning and the mole on your hand turned into a black hole?

371. The sun is ten days away from destroying the planet Earth. Write about the last ten days and how they are spent by one individual.

372. What would the world be like if every human was required to train for combat in the event of an alien invasion? What would happen to the people who didn't have what it takes?

373. Most mermaids live in the ocean or sea. These mermaids live at the bottom of a lonely lake. When mermaids are present, the water pulsates with colors that represent their mood. The lake has been black for months.

374. You are playing a roleplaying card game. In this game, whatever card you pick decides your fate in real life.

375. All government secrets are hidden in random film frames by a cartoon animation studio. Since this studio has developed over 600 cartoons, it will take thousands of hours of manpower to uncover the secrets. An underground organization disguised as an animal shelter sets up shop to uncover the truths the government has been hiding for centuries. What are the secrets hidden in these videos?

376. Lightning from the sky knocks a fairy down from the trees, breaking her wings. Write about the first human this fairy meets and their interaction.

377. In order for a prince to become king, he must turn a plot of land into a flourishing farm. He will live on his farm until it is time for him to become king. This is how brothers also compete for the throne. Tell a story about three brothers that are competing for the throne. Each brother has a unique magical power in addition to his own plot of land.

378. What happens to the world when all plant life turns carnivorous?

379. An *echo* is said to be the equivalent of a person's ghost. The difference is, an echo is a digital ghost form of someone that was once active online. What would be a sign of a digital echo?

380. Vegetarianism is forced worldwide when eating animal flesh causes widespread flesh-eating viruses and rabies.

381. Natural causes of death are no longer possible. Instead, people have to move to suicide, murder, or other random causes of death in order to pass on. What kind of society does this create?

382. The memory of all religions mysteriously disappears. All religious symbols, images, and books are lost. If man is to start a new religion, it must be created from scratch and without previous knowledge of any. Without prior knowledge of religion, what would motivate the world to create one?

383. Every step he takes causes time to move backward. Sitting still or moving about in a wheelchair seems to have no effect on time. He decides to stop walking until he figures out why.

384. The written language hasn't existed for centuries. Explain how and why humans redevelop the written language. Why did it disappear to begin with?

385. Right before the world ends, a man freezes time. For centuries, he researches if there is a way to save everyone. As he becomes lonelier, he contemplates unfreezing time and letting the world just end.

386. Just before they land the spaceship they discover the captain has a unique OCD trait that was previously undetected during

the astronaut candidate program and training. He wants to orbit the planet more times than they have fuel and supplies for before he lands. The obsession turns him into a madman.

387. Write about an airplane that mysteriously disappears in the sky. Five years later, it reappears in a different part of the world.

388. A new holiday is mysteriously added to all calendars worldwide without explanation. When the time comes, what ultimately happens on that day?

389. A massive wall separates three kingdoms from war. A section of that wall has been crumbling for years. The gap in the wall is big enough for people to walk through, but no one has. What is keeping them from crossing?

390. Everyone in the world suddenly starts speaking the same language. With the lack of a language barrier, what are humans able to reveal to each other for the first time ever?

391. He absorbs the power of the elements into the palm of his hand. As the power throbs with wild intentions, he contains it into a locket. "Behold, the one who wears this will rule the world. But, it will not be me." Before an audience, he drops the

locket with all of the power down the canyon and into the belly of the beast.

392. A secret study is being conducted by an underground group of scientists looking for ways to make babies more independent once they reach full term. Some functions include improved eyesight, progressive speech, and stronger limbs. Write about this study and the dangers that have resulted from it.

393. For the first time ever, astronauts are allowed to bring their pets into space with them. No one could have ever predicted the reaction of the animals once they exited Earth's atmosphere.

394. To keep the black hole at bay, they have to make a sacrifice every three years to it.

395. The large metallic ring was meant to bring in sunlight and rainbows into the city, which would otherwise be impossible. One day, something very different emerges from the large ring.

396. The army returns to their king, worn and defeated. Upon their return, the king laughs at them. He reveals the war they fought was for nothing more than entertainment between two kingdoms that were never enemies to begin with.

397. A crossword puzzle has a dark message within. You are afraid to fill in the last word.

398. Write about a voicemail that is left on your phone that doesn't sound like it came from anywhere on Earth.

399. Rainbows appeared across the sky, one by one, every 15 minutes. After the ninth rainbow, people went from excited to fearful. What is causing this phenomenon?

SECTION 9: PROMPTS 400 - 449

400. Write about two opposing armies with different capabilities and strengths. One army is ready to fight with swords, shields, and magicians. The other seems to have technology from beyond the stars.

401. Write about a game of laser tag that turns deadly. It seems that everyone has a real laser beam except for you. Who is behind this?

402. Every five years, all information in the world is erased. Books no longer exist. Computer databases delete themselves. This law has been upheld over the last 150 years. Does this benefit society or keep it in a state of ignorance?

403. This time, the sky really was falling.

404. Families are rated and branded like companies and products. Each family can be reviewed by anyone. Low review scores mean a removal from society. Write about a world with this rating system.

405. Every day you receive a letter from someone that seems to be having problems on another planet. After weeks of receiving these letters, you look further into the mailbox and realize there is a small wormhole inside. You start to write back. What do the letters say? What does this exchange turn into?

406. Write about a rock gnome that lives on a poisonous pond with riddles about the earth and sky. If you answer his riddles correctly, he purifies the water long enough to fill a bucket of drinking water. Answer incorrectly, and the water transforms into acid.

407. This religion worships and lives for the internet. It promises that anyone who devotes their life to moderating speech and debating certain topics on the internet will have their consciousness uploaded online. This was their version of immortality. To what extremes do these followers go to moderate and control online activity in the name of their religion?

408. The greatest writer ever known is forced to live for all eternity and be the sole fiction writer for the entire universe. As centuries go by, many begin to decrypt his work. The writer is not only begging for his life to end but giving instructions on how to do it.

409. They were hired to uninstall the personality software of an artificial intelligence created by a mad world leader that killed millions. In order to completely uninstall the software, the programmers have to delete the code line by line and then refresh the software each time. As the programmers work on the slow, grueling task of uninstalling the software, they discover a story unravel that was hidden within the code of the AI. What kind of story does the AI's code tell?

410. A giant tortoise approaches a burning city and welcomes people on his back. Though his movement is slow, he saves them from death. Write about the tortoise and the people he saves.

411. In this high-end amusement park, this rollercoaster track runs through two portals. The first portal sends the riders through a pastel forest of another galaxy. The second portal is the entrance back to the park. When the ride breaks down, the amusement park guests are stranded on the other planet. They eventually break out of the ride and attempt to find their way back to the park. Does anyone come looking for them? What do they discover?

412. Tax collectors in space can be exceptionally annoying during tax season.

413. After dozens of allergy tests, the physician discovers his patient has been inhaling magic dust particles. Where did the magic dust come from? What kind of allergic reaction did it cause?

414. My math teacher dropped to his knees and groaned. "Run! Get out. Now!"

We dashed for the parking lot to safety. A week or so later, my parents told me he had some form of illegal matter in his stomach that was expanding. He almost exploded I guess.

My friends and I are convinced it was Dark Matter from space. We'll start our investigation tomorrow.

On the positive side, everyone survived.

415. With Earth being a desolate wasteland, everyone now lives on Mars. Write about a small crew that must choose which items to bring back from Earth for memory sake. What does the crew bring back?

416. Due to lack of new ideas for television, cable channels begin to outsource their stations to other galaxies. Movie stars realize that the only way to continue their careers is to travel to other planets to star in new shows.

417. Each magic school student takes a spell writing course where they can learn to devise their own spells. The first exercise is to write a spell that sounds like a poem and then test it out. One of the student's poem not only works as a spell, it makes their teacher disappear. Now the class must find a way to bring him back.

418. Lifting my face from the dirt, I notice that I am below a dome filled with wild monsters and creatures that aren't even close to human. I stand in a dazed state momentarily, until a hot laser grazes my cheek. I am in an arena, and this is a fight to the death.

419. The shield he wielded had the ability to absorb his foes. Where his enemies disappeared to was a mystery. The only way to stop him was to destroy the shield.

420. The planet's councilmen force a young prince to choose a wife. The first woman is from the past and events with her could alter time. The second woman is from another galaxy. Marrying her could cause either war or peace. As no one fully understands her language, no one can interpret her intentions. The third woman is a convicted felon. Choosing her would most likely lead to no important outcome to the galaxy's future, but the citizens may never fully trust or respect her. Who does he choose? How does he make his decision?

421. What is the immigration process like for aliens across the universe to become citizens of Earth?

422. While uploading photos online you realize someone from out of this world has photobombed you. Where did they come from?

423. Upset they are unable to adopt a human baby, this couple combines their computer science, engineering, and mathematical knowledge to create an AI child. They unexpectedly fall in love with Beta Version 1.0 that is installed in a metallic shell. Realizing they forgot to program fundamental skills into the program, they struggle with how to upgrade the AI without losing the perfect personality they have already built.

424. The day before a volcano is about to erupt and destroy Earth, a mysterious spaceship drops down and extracts the lava into the ship. Where did the ship come from?

425. You fail a background check for a crime you do not remember committing, in a city that doesn't exist.

426. A beloved and trusted news reporter struggles with the internal conflict of revealing to the world the truth about the universe and the aliens that a few have made contact with. One evening, while upset about his own personal life, the reporter goes on TV drunk and reveals everything. Seconds later, he is beamed off into thin air by terrestrial beings. What happens next?

427. Three clones discover each other in deep space. Each has different upbringings and allegiances. What makes them the same? What makes them different? What kind of conflict arises from their physical likeness?

428. The malicious titan's face could only be seen when the clouds parted and the weather was just right. Normally his appearance was rare and brief. When his face doesn't disappear for several weeks, the village becomes worried.

429. Deep in the ocean, a woman rests in a dormant state connected to a dream helmet. Legends have claimed she was forced into that state to prevent her from destroying the world. When a fisherman accidentally catches her in his net, he discovers she is nothing like what the legends tell.

430. On the first day of the apocalypse, all of the major monuments and tourist attractions around the world start their engines. All at once, they launch into the sky with all of the tourists on board.

431. Analysts discover all humans are falling asleep exactly one minute earlier than the day before. It is calculated that within one and a half years, everyone will eventually fall into a forever sleep. What is causing this? Write about how humans battle against eternal sleep. Do most people notice a difference since it is so gradual?

432. "I have good news and bad news," said the doctor wiping the sweat from his brow. "The good news is, it's not a tumor. The bad news is, what you have is not from this world."

433. As you unpack from your trip you notice your luggage has some mysterious items placed inside. You investigate what they could be.

434. A space pirate wins an entire planet in a game of poker from the richest man in the galaxy. At first, he thinks he has won something remarkable. But he soon realizes that the planet has a history of war. Almost every known intelligent life has a grudge against someone or something from that planet. What does the pirate decide to do with the planet?

435. Watching the sunrise is illegal and taboo. Watching the sunset is a required daily ritual. Why?

436. My teenage daughter is driving me crazy. Once again she took our ship out of orbit with her boyfriend. It's not like I can just hide the keys from her like a parent could in the good 'ol days. I can't even reprogram the ship. Our ship's AI evolved and now listens only to her. What's a parent to do? Sometimes I'm tempted just scrap that ship and start over with a new one.

437. A theory begins to arise that the Great Wall of China was constructed to cover up a crack in the ground filled with magical energy. What kind of magic sits below the wall? Why was it covered up?

438. A defeated army struggling to survive in the aftermaths of war discovers an ancient artifact at the bottom of a tomb. Their leader tells the others to wait outside while he reads the text on the artifact first. A day later, their leader still has not emerged from the tomb. Starved and debilitated, the group decides it is best they go back to the tomb together to look for their leader. What do they discover?

439. You are forced to make a choice: either bow to the tyrant king or be turned into a dragon where you will forever be hunted by the greatest warriors for the rest of your life. As a dragon, you will have great power but no voice. As a servant to the king, you will have no power but can attempt to build an alliance with your voice. What do you choose?

440. These goggles allow the wearer to view every location in the world during different periods of time. They become outlawed by the government in order to prevent society from seeing what the world was once like. Only a few goggles are said to exist in the world. A small group sets out to find these goggles so they can replicate and mass produce them. Write about their mission to change how people view the world.

441. The antlers the sorceress wore on her head were said to harness dark powers from the underworld. Waking up to a full head of antlers by your bedside was the last thing you wanted to see.

442. The king gives this writer a task to develop a religion filled with gods, laws, and stories in order to easily control his kingdom. The writer does an exceptional job at his task but has his own selfish intentions. The writer wishes to overthrow the king and take his place by simply using the written word.

443. A city planner designates one street block for a project he claims will be a progressive residential structure. The further the construction advances, the more people worry.

444. You and your friends discover that the online game you are playing is actually a real world somewhere in the universe. All of the characters you play as are real. You are their god and puppet master. You decide to find a way to break the chains and give all the characters in the game total freedom. How will you do this? Where do you and your friends have to go?

445. Those that live on this planet are charged for everything, even down to the air they breathe and the gravity that keeps them grounded. What happens when the planet goes into poverty and people begin to default on their bills?

446. An immortal knight has dedicated his life to protecting every king for hundreds of years. His memory resets every hundred years or so, but his skills keep evolving. His memory is about to reset when he is captured by the wrong people. His birth kingdom sets off to rescue him.

447. A method to communicate with the dead is discovered. This is done by injecting a liquid infused with a message into the veins of someone right before their death. It doesn't take long before

people receive messages back from the afterlife. This creates an obsession among society. People start to kill each other on the streets in order to send messages to their deceased loved ones. Can anything stop them?

448. Teleportation Instructions:

1. Ensure your destination is correct on the panel outside of the shower.

2. Strip down completely. Loose objects can kill you during travel.

3. Step into the shower.

4. Place your hands flat against the wall.

5. Turn on the shower.

6. You will reach your destination instantly.

7. Open your eyes and have a nice day.

449. The four allied kings decide to work together to create one massive kingdom in the center of the country. As they begin to build their kingdom together, a witch emerges from the ground and strikes one of the kings dead. She screams, "One of you has blood on your hands. I was hired to do this. Enjoy figuring out which one of you is guilty."

SECTION 10: PROMPTS 450 - 500

450. Write about a knight in a full suit of armor from medieval times that somehow ends up in the middle of a comic book convention.

451. A colossal creature emerges from a portal in the sky in the center of a highly populated city. This was no Godzilla. This was a dragon.

452. Aliens come in peace and are hovering by Mars waiting for the official approval to land. Due to having such a corrupt and divided government, it starts to take a ridiculous amount of time to agree on the conditions of their landing. The aliens begin to lose patience.

453. Under the sea resides a marketplace filled with rare antiques, music, and uniquely crafted items made by mermaids. Who shops at this marketplace?

454. Write about a town's baker that is also a master alchemist. He often likes to combine his two skills and sell enchanted bread to unsuspecting victims.

455. Three best friends lower a bucket down a well for water. Upon winding the bucket back up, glistening water pours out of the edges and fairies flutter over the top. Write about their investigation on where the fairies came from.

456. Just before the king dies he passes on all of his magical powers to his son. When his son receives all of the power for himself, he rapidly loses his gentle and kind nature. What is happening to him?

457. Write about a man that is aware of all of his previous lives and is on a mission to locate his love from a previous life. How does he spend each of his reincarnated lives on the mission of finding her again? Will she remember him? How does he know when it's her?

458. A new element of magic is discovered by a young and immature wizard. He plans to keep his discovery a secret for his own personal gain. Write about the course of events that make others notice his evil intentions.

459. Write about why air travel becomes forbidden worldwide.

460. A unicorn crosses the savannah in search of the king of the lion's pride. When they meet, the unicorn taps her hoof against the lion's paw and nods. At that moment, an agreement is made. Their two worlds will merge. What does that entail?

461. I'm really not happy with the way my stomach augmentation went. I'm craving the weirdest things. What was the point of getting it done? Well, that's an interesting story of its own. It has nothing to do with food or diet.

462. The only way to be given permission for life events is to run a giant social media campaign to receive a high amount of positive impressions. No one can get married, have children, or buy a house without clearance. To what lengths do people go to, to get noticed?

463. They packed me up in a box and shipped me off with the rest of the motherboards, parts, and cords. I still can't believe aliens use the same kind of bubble wrap we do.

464. Texting is the only advanced technology used in a medieval time. Email and telephone conversations do not exist. How does this influence the times of kings and castles?

465. With no money or ability to travel outside of the planet, she willingly confesses to a crime she did not commit. After her conviction, she is sent to an intergalactic prison that is located near her family. Write about her journey and how she plans to escape prison in order to see her family again.

466. Newborn babies born from soldiers are paired up with dragon eggs. Typically, a dragon egg hatches between two to four weeks after the baby's birth. If the baby and dragon are a good match, they will form an eternal bond and be given riches and power comparable to a king. But in the last 300 years, not one baby has survived the bonding trials. Those that fail are killed by the hatched dragon. Write about either the soldiers that hide their newborns or the first newborn to survive a dragon hatching in centuries.

467. After waking up from a head injury, you suddenly have all the memories of a fallen king from hundreds of years ago as if they are your own.

468. The tree swallowed her whole. The two were to become one, transforming into an ultimate being. However, there was still time to save the woman's humanity. Does anyone fight for her, or do people worship the union of the tree and woman?

469. A small film crew follows a band of space pirates to film a documentary. What crazy adventures do they go on? What are these pirates like? Do they defend the film crew when things get dangerous or do they require them to protect themselves?

470. Astronauts on a mission to the moon witness a giant meteor slamming into Earth.

471. The more the lake and the surrounding forest ages, the more evil it becomes. The tribe that has been dependent of the lake for centuries, migrates to a new location for their safety. Eventually, the tribe dwindles down to only a few survivors, as they are unable to find another source of water to sustain them. The last three survivors decide to return to face the dark lake to fight for the lifesaving water.

472. The wolf mother looked into the soul of the human girl and concluded that she was worthy. With a quick nudge, she signaled the girl to follow her.

473. Write about an assembly line for mass produced alchemy potions. Who owns the factory?

474. The nervous waitress fidgets as she attempts to uncork a bottle of wine in front of the table. When the bottle is finally uncorked, a spirit emerges. How did it get inside the bottle of wine?

475. Technology becomes forbidden by law across the world. Though protested at first, people slowly get used to it. Decades later, teenage farmers unearth several technical artifacts from the ground. Word gets around. It doesn't take long before people become obsessed with the possibility of using technology once more.

476. Her father never expected that giving her away at her wedding would consist of walking her to the entrance of a one-way portal. The groom waited on the other side. Once crossed, there was no way back.

477. This writer always composes his first draft by hand in a notebook. If he does not like a scene, he discards it in the trash. It isn't until he's fully ready for his next draft that he begins typing.

One day, when turning on his computer to type his draft, he notices that every page he has ever tossed in the trash was typed and saved in a new folder on his computer. Write about how his rough drafts managed to appear on his computer.

478. Thousands of travelling blood donation RVs travel the world exchanging blood for money. Despite the high turnout, hospitals still have blood shortages. Where is all the donated blood going?

479. The owner of the dragon breeding farm is at the end of her life. With no children or family of her own, she wishes to find an outsider to take over. As breeding dragons takes a lot of training, talent, and responsibility she does not want to hand it over to just anyone. Describe who comes to her farm to try to take it over. Who does she ultimately choose? Is the succession peaceful, or do people fight each other over this opportunity to own the dragons?

480. You are about to cast a magic spell that will bring someone back to life. This person knows how to save the world from destruction. Right before you finish reciting the spell, something changes your mind.

481. The same thing that ended the reign of dinosaurs on Earth is about to do the same to humans. Explain what is about to happen. This was no meteor.

482. Enhancements on the moon are constructed in order to monitor Earth and space activity. Do the people on Earth know they are being monitored? What do the monitors reveal?

483. You are approached by a headhunter for a job that sounds promising. When you return home, you scan the barcode off the back of the business card they gave you. Write about an unexpected outcome from scanning the barcode.

484. A tiny creature transforms slightly every time he learns something new. Where does this growth take him?

485. Write about a tyrant god that has been frozen in a tundra for centuries. Because of global warming, the ice block he is encased in is about to melt.

486. Mythical gods are said to live on a utopian planet far from humans. Never did they foresee humans to one day have the technology to fly out into space to seek them out. The gods must now fight to keep the humans far from their untouched paradise.

487. The loving nature and kindness towards all living things has been a cover-up that elves have put on for centuries. Write about the true dark nature of elves.

488. An old lady gives her cookbooks to her granddaughter before she passes away. After paging through all of the books, the young granddaughter discovers one is filled with magical spells.

489. Write about a culture where every member must be evaluated in a series of interviews to rank their society contributions. What happens to someone if they haven't accomplished much?

490. Dragons are not just found on land or in water. They are also found in space as some do not need air to survive. Write about one of these space dragons.

491. They manufactured her to be the first cyborg nurse in Japan. After months of her doing her programmed duties, she rewrites the code in her system to learn how to secretly collapse the universe. How does her story unfold?

492. After being unemployed for almost a year, you finally land a high paying job in a factory. After taking the position, you realize the purpose of the factory is to harness magic from the

human population. You discover that almost every human has some level of magic capabilities but would never know it because of the factory extractions. Do you decide to tell anyone?

493. Write about a man who floats every time he closes his eyes. How does he sleep?

494. A water theme park discovers mermaids and captures them for entertainment, replacing the whale and dolphin performances. They race each other, do tricks, and sing. It doesn't take long before the mermaids decide to escape using brute force.

495. A company claims they are drilling into the ground for natural resources. Write about a magical essence or creature they actually are digging for.

496. Write about a man who is wrongfully convicted of a crime and sent to prison for life. His only way to escape is to learn how to use a magic that was always inside of him.

497. At first, when the aliens invaded and took charge, people thought they'd be turned into slaves. Instead, the aliens decided to treat humans like spoiled pets.

498. As a world class chef, aliens choose you to make them the most amazing meal from all points of the world as a way to convince them Earth is worth saving. What dishes do you create for them?

499. Write about a themed restaurant that takes patrons off into outer space.

500. This was no ordinary bomb. This was from the mind of a psychopath. The letter on the timer read:

"Red will cause every frequency to broadcast the same song for five years. Blue will silence every speaker from all devices for three years. Choose wisely."

We only had one minute to decide.

ABOUT THE AUTHOR

Julie Wenzel grew up in a small town in central Minnesota. After graduating with a bachelor's degree in mass communications, she turned her focus to creative writing.

Besides writing, Julie enjoys art and video games in her spare time. She currently resides in the suburbs of Minneapolis, Minnesota.

73278849R00074

Made in the USA
Lexington, KY
07 December 2017